KU-754-186

Out There?

MYSTERIES OF BODY & MIND

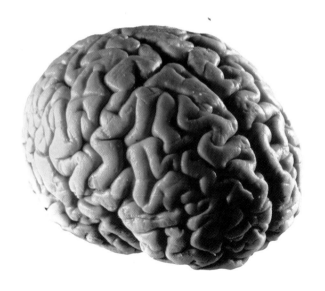

John Townsend

Raintree

www.raintreepublishers.co.uk
Visit our website to find out more information about **Raintree** books.

To order:
 Phone 44 (0) 1865 888113
 Send a fax to 44 (0) 1865 314091
Visit the Raintree Bookshop at **www.raintreepublishers.co.uk** to browse our catalogue and order online.

First published in Great Britain by Raintree Publishers, Halley Court, Jordan Hill, Oxford OX2 8EJ, part of Harcourt Education Ltd.
Raintree is a registered trademark of Harcourt Education Ltd.

© Harcourt Education Ltd 2004
The moral right of the proprietor has been asserted.

All rights reserved. No part of this publication may be reproduced, stored in a retrieval system, or transmitted in any form or by any means, electronic, mechanical, photocopying, recording, or otherwise, without either the prior written permission of the publishers or a licence permitting restricted copying in the United Kingdom issued by the Copyright Licensing Agency Ltd, 90 Tottenham Court Road, London W1T 4LP (www.cla.co.uk).

Editorial: Charlotte Guillain and Isabel Thomas
Design: Michelle Lisseter and Bridge Creative Services Ltd
Picture Research: Maria Joannou and Kay Altwegg
Production: Jonathan Smith

Originated by Ambassador
Printed and bound in China and Hong Kong by South China

ISBN 1 844 43221 1
08 07 06 05 04
10 9 8 7 6 5 4 3 2 1

British Library Cataloguing in Publication Data
A full catalogue record for this book is available from the British Library.

Acknowledgements
Page 04–05, Circus Images/Linda Rich; 04, Science Photo Library/Volker Steger; 05 mid, Fortean Picture Library/; 06–07, Corbis/; 06, Science Photo Library/Bernard Benoit; 07, Science Photo Library/Chris Bjornberg; 08 right, NHPA/Steve Robinson; 09, Science Photo Library/Damien Lovegrove; 08 left, Science Photo Library/Sue Ford; 10–11, Corbis/Tom Sanders; 10, Science Photo Library/CNRI; 11, PA Photos/; 12 right, Topham Picturepoint/; 12 left, Science Photo Library/Manfred Cage; 13, Topham Picturepoint/; 15, Fortean Picture Library/; 14, Advertising Archives/; 15 right, Fortean Picture Library/; 17 left, Science Photo Library/CC Studio; 16, Photodisc/; 17 right, Photodisc/; 18–19, The Sun/Daniel Kennedy; 18, Wellcome Trust Medical Photo library/; 19, Trevor Clifford/20–21, Corbis/; 20, Fortean Picture Library/; 21, Corbis/Nik Wheeler; 23 left, PA Photos; 22, Corbis/; 23 right, Corbis/Charles and Josette Lenars; 24–25, Topham Picturepoint/; 24, Topham Picturepoint/; 25, Corbis/; 27 left, Corbis/; 27 mid, Hulton Archives/; 27 right, Rex Features/; 27 right, Rex Features/; 26, Corbis/Jose Luis Pelaez; 29 left, Science Photo Library/Oscar Burriel; 29 right, Corbis/Jose Luis Pelaez; 28, Corbis/; 30–31, Topham Picturepoint/; 30, Science Photo Library/BSIP VEM; 31, Corbis/John Hulme, Eye Ubiquitous; 32, Science Photo Library/Oscar Burriel; 33, NHPA/; 34 right, Science Photo Library/Hank Morgan; 35 left, Science Photo Library/Hank Morgan; 35 right, Getty Images/Taxi; 34 left, Topham Picturepoint; 37 left, Science Photo Library/John Greim; 36, /Tudor Photography ; 37 right, Getty Images/Photographers Choice; 38–39, Corbis/; 38, Fortean Picture Library/; 40–41, Photodisc/; 40 top, Science Photo Library/Prof P Motta/Dept of Anatomy/University 'La Sapienza', Rome; 40, Science Photo Library/Custom Medical Stock Photo; 41, Corbis/; 42–43, Getty Images/Photographers Choice; 42, Topham Picturepoint/; 42, Topham Picturepoint/; 44–45, Science Photo Library/; 44, Fortean Picture Library/; 45, Fortean Picture Library/; 46–47, Fortean Picture Library/; 46, Corbis/Hulton; 47, Fortean Picture Library/; 48–49, Photodisc/; 48, Science Photo Library/Peter Menzel; 49, Science Photo; Library/Jean–Loup Charmet; 50–51, Science Photo Library/Adam Hart–Davis; 50, Science Photo Library/; 51, /R E Mawhood; Corbis/Steven Sutton/Duomo; 45, Science Photo Library/Martyn F Chillmaid; 52, Corbis/; 53, NHPA/Steve Robinson; 26 (Ohio twins story), Reader's Digest. Cover photograph reproduced with permission of Fortean Picture Library.

Every effort has been made to contact copyright holders of any material reproduced in this book. Any omissions will be rectified in subsequent printings if notice is given to the publishers.

Disclaimer
All the Internet addresses (URLs) given in this book were valid at the time of going to press. However, due to the dynamic nature of the Internet, some addresses may have changed, or sites may have changed or ceased to exist since publication. While the author and Publishers regret any inconvenience this may cause readers, no responsibility for any such changes can be accepted by either the author or the Publishers.

CONTENTS

DUDLEY PUBLIC LIBRARIES

L   47457

659375   SCH
         J001.94

Any words appearing in the text in bold, **like this**, are explained in the Glossary. You can also look out for them in the Weird words box at the bottom of each page.

BEING HUMAN

Secrets are locked inside our trillions of tiny cells:

- each minute, millions of our cells die
- we are making new cells all the time we are alive
- a tiny drop of blood has up to 5 million red cells and 15,000 white cells.

Mysteries hide inside all of us. Our bodies and minds are full of **puzzles**.

Just what makes us 'tick'? What makes all humans so different from each other?

All the time, scientists are finding new and amazing things about how our bodies work. Some of their discoveries could change our lives. Work on human **cells** is 'cracking the code' of how our **DNA** works. This could bring big changes to help fight disease.

The more we discover about the human body, the more we are amazed. Some people's bodies and minds can do very strange things. Some can go weirdly wrong.

Folds in the human brain mean a large amount of brain can be fitted in the skull. **>>**

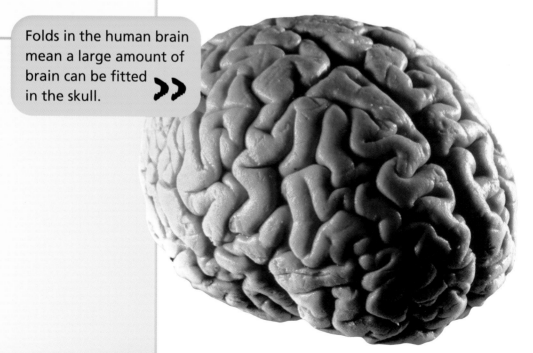

WEIRD WORDS

cells   tiny 'building blocks' that make up all living things
DNA   code locked in our genes that makes us who we are

AMAZING

The human brain is a wonder of science and no computer will ever match it. Our minds have many secrets and hidden powers. Some people's minds may even be able to pick up unknown signals.

Do these people have a gift or is it just nonsense? What really goes on inside our heads?

We have asked questions about our brains since we could first use them. This book asks questions, too. It may not give a lot of answers but it tells many strange stories. Some may be hard to prove but they have all been reported. They are often **mind-boggling**. These are just some of the mysteries that make us human.

Some bodies are very bendy. Don't try this at home!

FIND OUT LATER...

Do some people kill in their sleep?

Can people just burst into flames?

Do people really come back from the dead?

mind-boggling   hard to understand, baffling
puzzle   difficult and confusing problem

MYSTERIES OF THE BODY

MYSTERIES OF DNA

Life itself is the biggest mystery. We are still exploring the secrets of **DNA** and what makes us who we are. Each person on the planet is **unique**. How we behave has a lot to do with our **genes** and what happens to us as we grow up. That is why we are all so different. It takes 100,000 to 200,000 genes to create a human body.

Our **cells** still hold some secrets:
- How close are we to curing AIDS and cancer?
- Will we ever be able to stop ageing and even death itself?
- How will humans change in the future?

Just like DNA, every human fingerprint is individual. Even identical twins have different fingerprints.

DNA is a type of **acid** that holds all the instructions that make us all unique. The DNA of a single human cell holds enough information to fill 1000 encyclopaedias. If your DNA could be unwound, it would reach from the Earth to the Sun more than 400 times.

Bobby McCaughey and her seven babies.

acid   type of chemical
gene   set of instructions inside every cell

BIRTH

A human baby is born every 7 seconds. That is over 12,000 new humans each day.

Giving birth has its risks but some mothers **survive** having many babies. In 1997 it took Bobbie McCaughey from Iowa, USA, 16 minutes to give birth to a record seven babies. All four boys and three girls survived.

HOW MANY BABIES?

Leontina Albina from Chile gave birth to 55 babies between 1943 and 1981. This included nine sets of triplets and eleven sets of twins.

A Russian peasant in the 18th century had 69 babies. She had sixteen pairs of twins, seven sets of triplets and four sets of quadruplets between 1725 and 1765. A mystery or a **miracle**?

DID YOU KNOW?

- Babies are born without kneecaps. These develop between two and six years of age.

- Babies grow faster in the springtime.

- Our eyes stay the same size from birth, but our noses and ears never stop growing.

- Babies are born with over 300 bones; adults have 206.

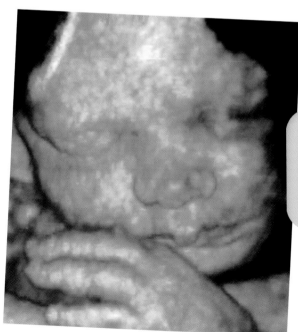

Scans have helped doctors to unlock many mysteries of how babies grow in the womb. ◀◀

miracle   something extraordinary or supernatural
unique   only one of its kind in the whole world

BLINKING

Each person spends about half an hour in every day blinking. That means that for a total of five years in a lifetime, we have our eyes shut while we are awake.

Women blink nearly twice as much as men. The average human blinks 6,205,000 times a year.

FUNNY FACES

Our faces say a lot about us. Small children soon learn to 'read' how faces show feelings. There are many different ideas about why humans smile and laugh. When we laugh, short bursts of air come out of our mouth and nose, at up to 112 kilometres (70 miles) per hour. The average person laughs about 15 times a day. That is not much, since laughing is supposed to do us good.

Scientists still have many questions about our bodies. Hundreds of mysteries **remain**. A funny example is, 'Why can't we tickle ourselves?'

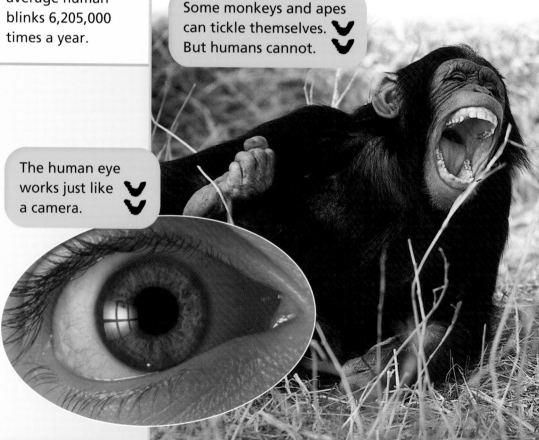

Some monkeys and apes can tickle themselves. But humans cannot.

The human eye works just like a camera.

myth   made-up tale, told over the years and handed on
pollen   powdery substance from flowers

HICCUPS

The world champion for hiccups was Charlie Osborne (1894–1991) of Ohio, USA. He started having hiccups in 1922 and stopped 68 years later.

A **pope** once died from the hiccups. Extreme hiccups like this are just another mystery of the human body.

NOT TO BE SNEEZED AT

People sneeze when the inside of their nose itches. The sneeze makes tiny droplets shoot out of the nose, clearing out any dust or **pollen**. Some sneezes can be faster than 160 kilometres (100 miles) per hour.

Three sneezing **myths**:
- when you sneeze, your heart stops
- if you sneeze more than thirteen times at once, you will die
- every time you sneeze you kill thousands of brain **cells**.

BLOOD FAST FACTS

- 15 million blood cells are destroyed in the human body every second.
- Each human blood cell travels 96,000 kilometres (60,000 miles) around the body in a day.
- Our hearts pump about 180 million litres of blood in a lifetime.

It is impossible to sneeze with your eyes open! **◀◀**

pope head of the Roman Catholic Church
remain stay the same or be left behind

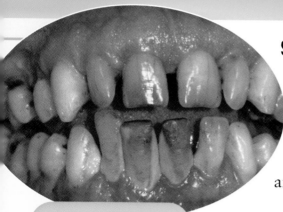

SURVIVAL

Our bodies are amazing machines but they can be easily broken. Some very fit people have died after a simple fall. Yet others **survive** terrible accidents and amaze their doctors.

Teeth are the only part of our skeleton that is not covered by flesh and skin. They need special care.

CAN YOU EXPLAIN IT?

- Bob Aubrey from Canada was blind – until he tripped over his guide dog and his sight came back.
- Pedro Alvarez from Chile was also blind. He had a bad tooth so the dentist pulled it out. When Pedro opened his eyes, he could see.

OUCH!

Mark Mongillo was a 22-year-old skydiver from Florida. In 1977 he made his twelfth jump from an aeroplane. But this time it went wrong. At 900 metres above the ground, both parachutes failed and he fell at great speed. He hit solid ground, bounced twice and landed in a ditch. He was still alive. He broke his leg and needed **surgery**, but he survived.

revive   bring back to life

BOUNCING BACK

In World War 2 many men fell from burning aircraft. Most were killed but some lived to tell the tale. A Russian pilot had to jump out of his plane and fell over 7000 metres without a parachute. Deep snow broke his fall and he survived, even though he broke many bones.

In 1944 Nicholas Alkemade's plane exploded over Germany. His parachute was blown right off. He fell without it, from 6000 metres. 'I felt a strange peace away from the heat,' he said. 'If this was dying it was nothing to fear.' He fell into fir trees and then into deep snow. He got up and walked away.

In November 2000, magician David Blaine stood for 58 hours in a six-tonne block of ice. In 2003 he survived without food for 44 days.

In 1985 a toddler called Michael Troche walked outside in pyjamas one night. The temperature was −16 °C. He was found hours later, frozen stiff in the snow. His heart had stopped. He was dead but doctors **revived** him. After days of intensive care and **skin grafts**, he survived.

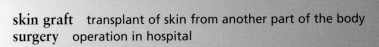

skin graft   transplant of skin from another part of the body
surgery   operation in hospital

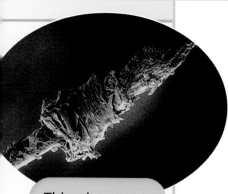

This microscope picture shows the root of a human hair.

EXTREME

Some people's bodies get into the record books. They are mysteries to **medical science**.

LARGER THAN LIFE

Robert Wadlow was born in Alton, Illinois in the USA in 1918. He was a normal-sized baby, but soon he grew... and grew. At the age of 13 he was over 2 metres tall.

HAIRY FACTS

- Blonde-haired people have more hair than dark-haired people.
- The eyelashes that fall from a human eye in a lifetime would measure over 30 metres if put end to end.
- Beards are the fastest growing hair. They can grow up to 10 metres in a lifetime!

In this photo, Robert Wadlow is shown with two of his relatives.

He reached 2.72 metres – the tallest man ever. He was only 22 when he died of an infected foot blister in 1940. **Antibiotics** that could have saved him were discovered a few months later. It took twelve men to carry Robert Wadlow's coffin. His grave and a life-size statue are at Alton, USA.

QUITE A SIZE

Robert Earl Hughes was born in 1926, also in Illinois. He was 3.15 metres round his chest. At the age of six he weighed 92 kg. When he died in 1958, he weighed 468 kg.

He was buried in a huge piano case that was lowered into the grave by a crane.

BIGGER STILL

The heaviest woman ever recorded was Rosalie Bradford from Pennsylvania USA. In 1987 she was 43 years old and weighed 544 kilograms. Doctors said she would die if she did not lose weight. After a strict diet, Rosalie had lost over 400 kilograms by 1994. Then she started helping other overweight people to diet.

THE SHORTEST COUPLE

Douglas Breger da Silva and Claudia Rocha were married in Brazil in 1998. She was taller than him by 3 cm. He was just 90 cm. That is the height of a standard sink unit. They are the shortest married couple in the world.

At just 70 cm tall, this Hungarian circus performer claims to be the world's shortest man. >>

CIRCUS OF THE BODY

Just 100 years ago, people with unusual bodies were often put in a circus in a **freak show** for people to stare at. Some **'exhibits'** had extra limbs. Others were twins who were joined together.

EXTRAORDINARY

Human bodies come in all shapes and sizes but most are similar in the way all the parts fit together and grow. But not always...

THE ELEPHANT MAN

John Merrick lived in London in the 19th century. He had a rare disease that made his **cells** grow out of control. His body and head grew out of shape. His skin became 'elephant-like'. People were cruel to him because he looked so different, so he wore a mask. He was a brave and gentle man but he was put into a **freak show**. A doctor saved him and tried to help, but John died in 1890 at the age of about 30.

UNUSUAL BODIES

A teenager was stabbed in Hungary in 1997 and doctors said he would die. The knife went into his chest, just where his heart should have been. Luckily for him, his body was a bit odd. His heart was on the right of his chest instead of on the left. His unusual body saved his life.

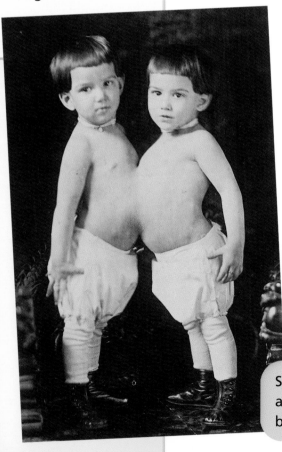

Siamese twins Guadalupe and Josefina were born in Cuba in 1912.

In China, a man called Deng has three eyes. His extra eye is on the side of his head, with an eyebrow and lashes. Another Chinese man had three tongues. In 1998 doctors took away the two extras so he could speak. So not all human bodies are the same.

Frank Lentini joined a circus in 1898 when he was nine. He had an extra leg at the base of his spine. He was a star as the 'Three-Legged Wonder' in the Wild West show. He died in Florida in 1966.

This photo of an Arab with extra fingers and toes was taken in 1933.

Adverts like this were common 100 years ago. Are we more caring today?

FRED^k MELVILLE'S
EXTRAORDINARY NOVELTY PLAY OF HUMAN INTEREST

THE UGLIEST WOMAN ON EARTH

freak show   place where people with unusual bodies used to be put on show

MYSTERIES OF THE MIND

DID YOU KNOW?

- The human brain has about 100 billion nerve cells.
- Nerve signals from the brain travel as fast as 270 km/h (170 mph). That is faster than a high-speed train!
- About 85 per cent of your brain's weight is water.
- Every minute 0.85 litres of blood pass through the brain.

The human brain must be one of the wonders of the world. The mystery of what goes on inside our heads has puzzled us from the start of time.

INSIDE OUR HEADS

Your brain is a grey mass that looks like a big soft walnut. How is it able to do so much? Not only can it think, love, sleep, dream and imagine, it can sometimes have strange powers. And yet we only use a fraction of our brains.

In relation to the size of our bodies, we have bigger brains than animals. The human brain is packed with about 15 billion spidery nerve **cells,** called neurons. An insect has only 100,000 neurons.

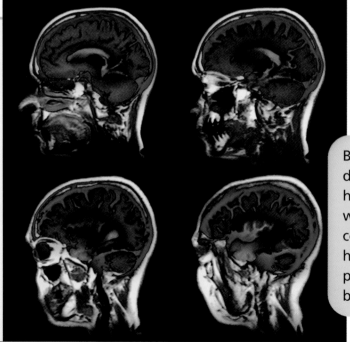

Brain scans help doctors discover how the mind works. Different colours show how active each part of the brain is. **««**

WEIRD WORDS

mental   to do with the mind
pressure   force per unit of area

UNDER PRESSURE

In 1998 sportsman Hayden McGlinn hit his head and fell in Western Australia. A doctor watching the game went to help. He thought there was a blood clot on Hayden's brain. The doctor had to act fast. He needed to drill a hole in Hayden's head to reduce the **pressure** on his brain. It was **urgent**, so the doctor ran to a shed and found some rusty tools. They would have to do! He drilled a hole in Hayden's skull and hoped for the best. It worked and Hayden made a full recovery. The tools are now on show in a nearby pub.

When the Moon is full, it is said that doctors treat more people with mental illness.

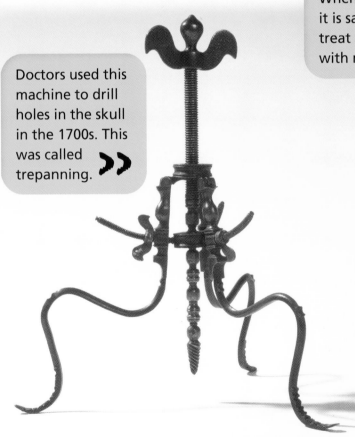

Doctors used this machine to drill holes in the skull in the 1700s. This was called trepanning. **>>**

THE MYSTERY OF THE MOON

Years ago, people with **mental** problems were called lunatics. The word 'lunatic' means 'of the Moon'. That is because the cycles of the Moon are supposed to affect human behaviour.

AMAZING RECOVERY

In 1848 an explosion blasted a metal rod into Phineas Gage's left cheek. It flew through his skull and brain and came right out of the top of his head. But he lived for another 13 years. His skull and the rod are now in a museum in Boston, USA.

BRAIN SURVIVAL

Just like our bodies, our brains are **fragile**. Our skulls have to protect them from all kinds of knocks. Even gentle knocks can harm the brain. But some brains have **survived** the most terrible injuries.

A NASTY HEADACHE

In 1981 a man in Boston, USA, drove into a tree. A steel pole in the back of his truck shot forward. It went straight through the back of his head and came out above his left eye. Doctors had to remove the pole very carefully. The man's brain was damaged and he had speech problems for a while. But before long he was up and about again. What an amazing brain!

A person can even survive getting shot in the head if the bullets land in the right place. **>>**

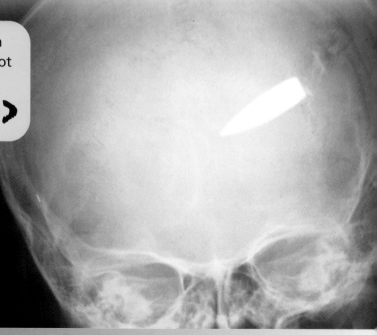

fragile   easily broken or damaged

A TOUGH NUT

David Wright was a builder in Toronto. In 1983 he fell from his ladder while holding a power drill. As he hit the floor, the drill went into his head. It got stuck. He knew he could not pull it out as it could cause major brain damage. He went indoors to look in a mirror. He put the drill into reverse and switched it on. The drill spun and he slowly pulled it out of his brain. Then he went to hospital. Although there was a deep hole in his brain, there was no major damage. He must have had a bit of a headache, though!

This X-ray shows a harpoon spear stuck in the head of a 15-year-old boy from Berkshire, UK. He survived!

JUST LOOKING

In 1998 a man walked into a police station in Ohio in the USA. He had a wire sticking out of his head. He said he had wanted to find his brain. He had drilled a 15 cm hole in his skull and stuck the wire inside. There must have been a full Moon that night!

MIND MESSAGES

Can we really pick up warning signals that tell us how to save our lives? Some people swear they hear messages 'from beyond'. In some cases it has been life-saving.

MIND OVER MATTER

Some people train their minds to blot out pain. They seem to put themselves into a **trance**.

These priests at a village temple in Madras, South India, do fire-walking. Afterwards their feet are not blistered or **scorched**. They feel no pain.

NARROW ESCAPE

In 1985 Mrs Slater was about to change her baby's nappy on her kitchen table when she had a strong feeling. She knew she had to take her baby into the next room, which she did. It was just as well. A lorry crashed through her fence and spilt 12 tonnes of gravel straight through her kitchen window – all over the kitchen table. It was just as well she got the message!

WEIRD WORDS   trance   sleep-like state

MENTAL WARNING

In Wiltzhelden, Germany in 1972, a boy called Joachim ran into the kitchen and shouted, 'Mum – quick, get out!' He looked very worried, so his mother ran out of the house. As soon as they got outside, a gas explosion wrecked their house. As they stared at the rubble, Joachim could only say, 'I don't know how I knew. I just knew I had to get everyone out of the house. It was like a voice in my head.' Another strange case of a 'mind message'? Such reports seem fairly common. Who knows where the voice comes from?

A mysterious helper or a lucky escape?

NIGHTMARE MESSAGE

In 1987 Wendy Finkel was killed in a car crash near Point Mugu in California. Police went to tell her mother, but she already knew what had happened. The night before she had dreamed that her daughter was killed in a crash. The dream happened at exactly the time her daughter died.

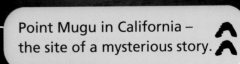
Point Mugu in California – the site of a mysterious story.

E.S.P.

E.S.P. stands for **Extra Sensory Perception**. It is when people know something has happened without being told. People do more than just read minds. They seem able to tune in to **mental** signals.

Some people can do this so often that they are said to have **psychic** powers.

THE POWER OF THE MIND

Sometimes the police need extra help to **solve** a crime. Mind-power has found answers to murder mysteries.

THE CASE OF THE YORKSHIRE RIPPER

In 1979, a killer was on the loose in Britain. He had killed twelve women. Police asked the **psychic** Nella Jones if she could 'see' the killer. She had a vision and said his name was Peter and he drove a lorry. She was sure he lived on a hill in Bradford, with a 6 on the door. She also saw a letter 'C' on his lorry.

Peter Sutcliffe was later **convicted**. The name 'Clark' was on the door of his lorry. His house was on a hill – number 6 Garden Lane, Bradford. Nella was spot on!

This photo of Peter Sutcliffe is world-famous. **>>**

convicted   found guilty of a crime
psychic   showing unusual powers of the mind

DEADLY FEELING

In 1958, Fred Trusty was building steps on a hill near his house in Painesville, Ohio, in the USA. He suddenly 'felt odd'. He dropped his tools and looked over at a nearby pond. He saw nothing unusual so he got back to work. The odd feeling came back. The pond seemed to draw him to it. He went to look and saw a boy's cap in the water. He was just in time to dive in and save his son Paul, who was drowning at the bottom of the pond.

Just what went on in Fred's mind to warn him? It is yet another mystery of the mind.

PSYCHIC RESCUE

In 1997 a plane disappeared over the jungle in Colombia, South America. A search party found nothing. Ismael Aldana's two children had been on board the plane. She went to a psychic who told her where the plane had crashed. They soon found it there – and her two children were still alive.

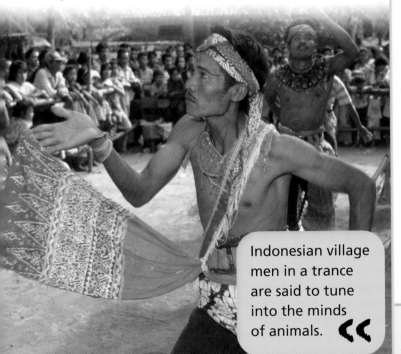

Indonesian village men in a trance are said to tune into the minds of animals.

MIND-BENDING

Can thinking make things happen? Can brain waves affect solid objects? There are plenty of stories that suggest this is possible.

Some hypnotists use a swinging watch to help put patients into a trance.

POWER OVER THE MIND

Hypnosis has always been something of a mystery. It can help to 'unlock secrets of the memory' and to treat stress and other problems. It makes people laugh when used as TV entertainment. But what about the dangers of being under someone's control?

SPOON-BENDING

People like Uri Geller use their **mental** powers on stage and television.

When Uri was five, a spoon in his hand curled up and broke for no reason. When he grew up he bent spoons for a living. He went on television, bending spoons and forks just by stroking them. Some people watching said spoons near their television sets also bent.

Uri once stopped a cable-car and an escalator using just mind power. In 1984, he rubbed a computer disk clear with 'brain-waves', in front of computer experts. ▶▶

hypnosis   putting someone into a trance or sleep
irrational   for no clear reason

MIND POWER

In Indiana in the 1880s, a man called Spencer did 'magic' tricks and mind-reading on the stage. After his act one night, John Harmon asked for help. John lived with his mother and three sisters. All their savings had just vanished. He asked Spencer to help them track the money down.

As only the family had known where the money was kept, Spencer tried **hypnosis** on each one in turn. In a **trance**, one of John's sisters went to a pile of logs. The money was buried underneath. She had no idea why it was there. She swore she must have hidden it when sleepwalking.

PHOBIA

A **phobia** is an **irrational** fear. Some people have a phobia of heights, water or small spaces. Often there seems to be no reason. Hypnosis can help people get to the **root** of the problem and face their fears. That is mind-bending!

A fear of spiders is called arachnophobia. Many sufferers claim to have been cured by hypnosis.

phobia   real fear and dread of a particular thing or place
root   real reason or cause

A WEIRD COINCIDENCE IN WALES

The Menai Straits are a stretch of sea in North Wales.

On 5 December 1664 a ship sank there. Hugh Williams was the only survivor.

On 5 December 1785 another ship sank. The only survivor was called Hugh Williams.

On 5 December 1860 yet another ship sank. The only survivor was called Hugh Williams.

Hugh must be a lucky name!

Identical twins often make identical decisions – even if they live miles apart. >>

AGAINST ALL THE ODDS

What is the chance of two people having the same idea at the same time? Maybe it is not so strange – unless it happens a lot…

COINCIDENCE

Twin boys were separated at birth in Ohio, USA. Different families adopted them. Unknown to each other, both families named the boys 'James'.

Both boys grew up not knowing they had a brother. Both were good at carpentry and drawing. Both married women named Linda. Both had sons named James Alan. Both divorced their wives and married other women – both named Betty. Both owned dogs named Toy. The brothers met for the first time when they were forty and found out about their similar lives.

coincidence   two or more strange things that happen at the same time or together

PRESIDENT LINCOLN AND PRESIDENT KENNEDY

There are many strange links between these two US presidents, even though there were 100 years between them. The **coincidences** are spooky.

Lincoln was shot in a theatre and his killer ran to hide in a warehouse. Kennedy's killer shot him from a warehouse and ran to a theatre.

Both men were killed on a Friday after being warned by their staff. A woman called Miss Kennedy warned Lincoln not to go to the theatre, and one called Miss Lincoln warned Kennedy not to go to Dallas.

Some coincidences can be embarrassing, such as turning up at a party dressed the same as someone else!

After their deaths, men called Johnson replaced both presidents. One Johnson was born in 1808 and the other was born in 1908.

JUST CHANCE?

John and Arthur Mowforth were twins who lived 120 kilometres (80 miles) apart in the UK. On 22 May 1975, both fell ill from chest pains. Both men were rushed to separate hospitals at the same time. Both died of heart attacks just after arrival.

Lincoln became president in 1860 and was assassinated on a Friday.

Kennedy became president in 1960 and was assassinated on a Friday.

MYSTERIES OF SLEEP

SLEEPING LIKE A BABY

- Newborn babies need to sleep for about 18 hours a day.

- Toddlers need about 12 hours a day.

- From about the age of 8 up to your late teens, you need 8 to 9 hours of sleep a night.

Strange things happen to our brains when we sleep. Scientists know sleep is **vital**, but they still do not know what sleep really is. It is not just rest, because our minds keep working. In fact, people can do weird things when they are asleep. Lack of sleep can be harmful to us because our bodies do repair jobs while we sleep.

SLEEP WALKING

Sleepwalking is more common in children, especially boys between the ages of 5 and 12. It tends to run in families, but it does not mean there is a medical problem. Doctors still do not know why some people go walk-about at night.

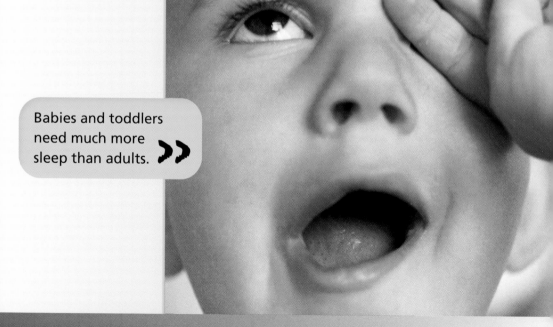

Babies and toddlers need much more sleep than adults. >>

evidence   information available to help prove if something is true or false

MURDER BY SLEEP?

In 1845 Albert Tirrell murdered Maria Bickford in her bed in Boston, USA. He then started fires in the house. Perhaps he was trying to hide the **evidence**. He told police it was not him as he had been asleep in the house at the time.

In court, he told the jury he was a sleepwalker. He said he must have been sleepwalking when he killed Maria and lit the fires. It did not take the jury long to agree. They said Albert was not guilty of murder.

Several people since have claimed that their crimes were committed in their sleep – and some have got away with it.

ARE YOU GETTING ENOUGH SLEEP?

- Some adults can manage on 4 hours of sleep a night. Most sleep for 7 to 8 hours. This helps the brain recharge, but it may also help to 'flush out' unwanted chemicals in our bodies.

- Older adults often sleep less, perhaps because they have less 'sleep **hormone**'.

hormone   chemical in the body that makes things happen
vital   really important

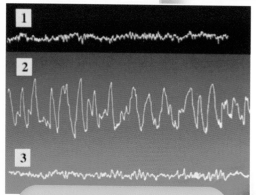

1 Brain waves when awake
2 Brain waves during normal sleep
3 Brain wave pattern while dreaming

BRAIN WAVES

An EEG scan records brain waves. Scientists have found that the brain waves of a dreaming person are much more like those when they are awake than sound asleep.

THE WORLD OF DREAMS

No one really knows why we dream. Maybe our brains are sorting all the information from the day. Or is it more than that? Our dreams may be telling us about the deeper parts of our minds, our fears and **desires**.

People have always tried to make sense of dreams. In **ancient** times, dreams were taken very seriously. A dream was a message or warning. People thought it told them about the future. It is common to dream we are flying, falling or doing something totally **bizarre**. Just what are our brains up to?

We all dream most nights even though we do not always remember.

ancient   from a long time ago
bizarre   very strange or weird

WARNINGS

People sometimes dream about plane crashes and murders just before they happen. Spooky!

Abraham Lincoln dreamed about his death and told other people about it. He was killed soon afterwards.

The writer Mark Twain dreamed about his brother's body in a coffin. He saw white and red flowers. Mark was so worried by this, he got up to find out where his brother was. His brother was on a steamship near Memphis but within hours the ship exploded. Mark rushed to Memphis to see his brother. It was too late. His brother was dead and lying exactly as he had been in the dream. Even the flowers were just like the ones in Mark's dream.

A LIFE-CHANGING DREAM

In 1991 a poor food-seller in Thailand had a dream about ghosts. The ghosts gave her some lottery numbers. The next day she spent her last coins on a lottery ticket. All the numbers came up and she won £150,000!

Dreaming of the winning lottery numbers might change your life! **<<**

TEN WAYS TO HELP SLEEP

- lie facing north
- wiggle your toes
- rub your stomach
- do deep breathing
- count sheep
- take a warm bath
- listen to slow music
- drink warm milk
- drink herb tea
- avoid naps in the day

BAD SLEEP

Nightmares are bad enough. Some people have bad dreams every night and wake up **exhausted**. But what if you *cannot* sleep? What if your brain never closes down?

A **Buddhist monk** called Dawa did not sleep properly for almost 80 years. His pulse was always very slow even though he was wide awake. Doctors were amazed that he could stay healthy without real sleep.

BAD NIGHTS

Thi Le Hang from Vietnam claims she has not slept since her son was born in 1965. She said, 'I go to the gym every day but I never feel tired. Even sleeping pills don't help. I'd like to have a good night's sleep. Just once!'

Some people lie awake all night without sleeping. **》》**

WEIRD WORDS   Buddhist monk   man who devotes his life to following the religion of Buddha

SLEEPLESS DEATH

An Italian man had very bad **insomnia**. He could only sleep for one hour every night. He had bad dreams that woke him up. Sleep is important to keep the memory working and the man began to lose his memory.

After a year of not sleeping, he died from 'burn-out'. Doctors then cut open his brain. There was a lot of damage. Lack of sleep seemed to have destroyed many nerve cells. Or was it the lack of nerve cells that stopped him sleeping? It seems other members of his family had the same mystery illness.

- Do not drink tea or coffee late at night.
- Get regular exercise but not late at night.
- Do not eat a heavy meal late at night.
- A light snack before bed may help sleep.
- If it is noisy, use earplugs.

Counting sheep in your mind is supposed to relax you and help you sleep.

exhausted   weak from being very tired and losing all energy
insomnia   inability to sleep

33

TWILIGHT WORLD

Some people fall asleep in strange places just because they are so tired.

WHEN SLEEP TAKES OVER

Some people cannot help falling asleep. Their brain keeps cutting out. They fall asleep in odd places. Doctors think it is a chemical problem in the brain. Sometimes a victim will 'close down' and even seem dead. This problem is called narcolepsy.

Allison Burchell is lucky to have reached her 65th birthday. She has a very rare disease. It makes her pass out now and again and she goes into a deep **coma**. Any shock can bring it on. Sometimes laughing or crying can make her faint, but she looks as if she is dead. She goes pale and her pulse is so faint it is hard to find. She does not seem to be breathing. But she is – and she knows exactly what is going on around her. She can hear but she just cannot move. It can take many hours for her to 'wake up'. Allison has been sent to the **mortuary** several times.

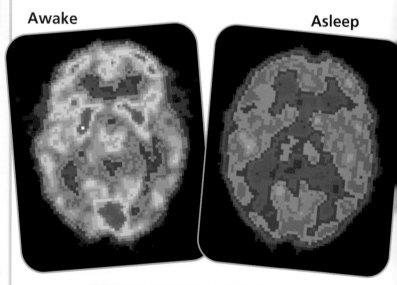

Awake   **Asleep**

A brain scan shows active areas in red and yellow and inactive areas in blue and purple. During deep sleep, most of the brain is 'switched off'.

coma   very deep sleep where the brain cannot be woken
declare   announce news in an official way

NEARLY THE END

Allison was first **declared** dead when she was 16. She fell out of her seat at the cinema. People rushed her to hospital. The nurses thought she was dead. She could hear the nurses talking as they put her on a slab near some dead bodies. Much later she was able to sit up. The attendant screamed and ran out of the room.

Years later Allison moved from England to Australia. She fell down in the street and the police thought she was dead. Her son had to beg them not to zip her up in a body bag. In the last few years, drugs have stopped the attacks.

BRAIN MYSTERY

Sometimes the brain's nerve cells are damaged by a build-up of a **protein**. The **neuron** connections stop working properly, so thinking becomes muddled. This is called Alzheimer's disease. It has always been a mystery but doctors hope to be able to treat the disease soon.

mortuary room where dead bodies are kept before they are buried

WAKING UP AT A FUNERAL

In 1977 a Spanish woman called Inez Martinez fell off her moped. Doctors said she was dead. But during her funeral a few days later, noises came from the coffin. The priest opened the lid. Inez was still alive and she was rushed away to hospital.

Some coma patients have had a lucky escape!

COMA

The Greek word *koma* means 'deep sleep'. Nothing will wake someone who is in a **coma**. An injured brain swells and presses against the inside of the skull. This cuts off the blood and oxygen to brain **cells**. It takes less than 20 minutes for cells to starve and die.

Many people who wake up from a coma say they remember some of their time asleep. The longest someone was in a coma and woke up was 37 years.

In 2003 a 24-year-old German woman woke from a seven-year coma after she was wheeled to a concert. The band had been her favourite as a teenager. It must have been a lively concert!

fatal   causing or ending in death

BACK TO LIFE

Mrs Jones fell into a deep coma at home in Yorkshire, in the UK. Her doctor said she was dead. Her family were shocked. All they could do was call the **undertaker** and the police. As Mrs Jones's body was about to be put into a body bag, a policeman thought he saw her leg move. He took her pulse and gave her the kiss of life. She was breathing.

They rushed her to hospital. Two days later she woke up from her coma. She had been so close to going in a body bag. In 2000 she was awarded £40,000 for the almost **fatal** mistake.

SPOOKY CHESS

In 1996 two workers were on the night shift in a **mortuary** in Cuba. They were playing chess when suddenly a body sat up and grabbed one of the chess pieces. Miguel Garcia had woken up on the slab. He later got better in hospital – but he lost the chess game!

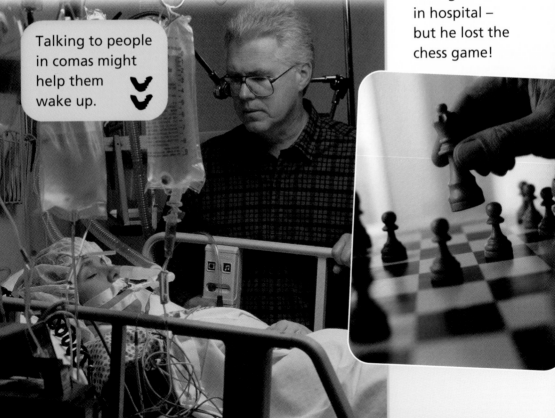

Talking to people in comas might help them wake up.

LEAVING THE BODY

Some people say they have been asleep and floated out of their body. They say they rose above their bed and hung in the air. Some said a silver cord tied them to their body below. Nobody knows why some people have these out-of-body experiences.

BETWEEN LIFE AND DEATH

Thousands of people say they have come back from the dead. Their hearts stopped and it was a fight for doctors to **revive** them. These people were brought back to life after a few minutes. Many just get on with their lives again. But some people always remember how they left their dead body and looked down on the doctors at work. These people have had near-death **experiences**.

Nearly all these people say they felt at peace as they floated to another world. Many people remember travelling down a tunnel towards a bright light. But they were called back and re-entered their body on the bed.

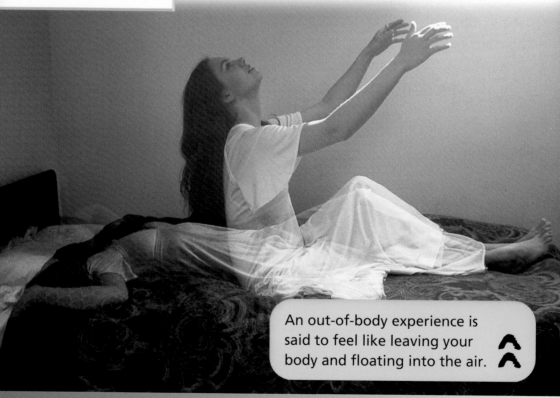

An out-of-body experience is said to feel like leaving your body and floating into the air.

experience   event in which someone is personally involved

A MYSTERIOUS JOURNEY

In 1997 a 78-year-old man's heart stopped in hospital. His heart was started again in a while, after electric-shock treatment. He wrote his story but did not give his name.

This story is **typical** of many people's experiences.

'I lay on the bed as someone led me to a big bright star. I could hear singing, which got louder as I moved nearer. I saw thousands of people with their arms open to greet me. I was about to enter the star when a voice said, 'Go back.' I could see three people dragging me back. I found out later there had been three nurses reviving me.'

MORE COMMON THAN YOU MAY THINK

- Over 10,000 near-death experiences have been recorded round the world.
- It seems to make no difference what a person's religion is, or even if they believe in life after death.
- In nearly all cases, people say they no longer fear dying.

What happens in a person's mind as they are brought back to life?

MYSTERIES OF LIFE AND DEATH

MYSTERY BODY

A man was found dead on Dartmoor in 1975. Tests could not find out why he died. He was dressed in a smart suit. He had a map, cash and a bottle of sweet and sour sauce. He had poison pills on him, but none in his body. His death was never solved.

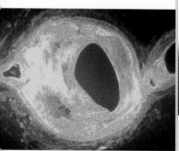

Blocked arteries can be a cause of sudden death. A build up of fatty material is shown in yellow. It leaves much less room for blood to flow through.

Every day people die for no **apparent** reason. One minute they seem to be fine but the next they are dead. The mystery is often **solved** at a **post mortem**.

SUDDEN DEATH

Some fit sportspeople die after a slight bump during a game. Why do they die when their heart is so healthy? One idea is that the timing of the bump is very important. If someone is hit on the chest at the exact second of a heart's beat, they could die. Matthew Messing was 16 in 1995 when he suddenly died after a bump in an ice hockey game in the USA. It may just have been bad timing.

apparent   seeming to be the case

SLOW DEATH FROM A VERY SLOW BULLET

This story from Texas seems so amazing that it must have been a real problem for police to solve.

Henry Ziegland left his girlfriend in 1893. She was so upset that she asked her brother to shoot Henry. The bullet missed and went into a tree. Henry got up and carried on with his life for another 20 years. The tree kept growing.

In 1913 Henry wanted to cut down the tree but it was too big for an axe. He decided to use dynamite instead. The explosion fired out the bullet from 20 years ago. It shot straight into Henry's head and killed him.

MYSTERY OF BEATING DEATH

People live longer now than ever before. About 25,000 people in the world are over 100 years old.

The oldest person on record was Jeanne Calment, who died in 1997 aged 122 years, 164 days.

What are the secrets of active long life? ◀◀

post mortem examination of a dead body to find the cause of death

THE BURNING QUESTION

How can a human body **ignite** by itself? After all, our bodies are mostly water. Apart from a little fat and gas, there is not much inside us that will burn. It seems impossible that anyone should even make a spark.

The ashy remains of this 69-year-old woman were found in 1958.

BODIES THAT BURST INTO FLAMES

One particular mystery has puzzled the world for years. It is very rare but it raises many questions. Why do some people suddenly burst into flames? Do they have a built-in fuse? In the past 300 years, there have been over 400 reports of people going up in smoke for no reason.

THE MYSTERY OF THE BURNING DOCTOR

Dr John Bentley was 92 years old. He was in good health even though he walked with a frame. In 1966, a man called to read the meter at Dr Bentley's home. The man let himself into the basement, where he saw a strange haze of light blue smoke.

ignite   catch fire

FOUND

There was much more smoke upstairs. Dr Bentley's burnt remains were in the bathroom. All that was left of him was the lower half of his right leg and slipper. A pile of ashes was on the floor. The rubber tips of his walking frame were still there and the nearby bath was hardly **scorched**.

NEVER SOLVED

Did Dr Bentley set himself on fire with his pipe? This was not possible because his pipe was still by the bed in the next room. To this day no one knows what really happened. Why would an old man burn to ash while his house was left unmarked?

ALL CASES ARE SIMILAR

- Most of the victim's body and clothes become ash.
- Only small parts of the body, such as an arm or a foot, remain unburned.
- Only objects to do with the body burn; the fire never spreads to other parts of the room.

The foot of Dr Bentley was all that remained. His walking frame was hardly damaged. **≪**

scorch   burn and brown the surface only

BACK TO FRONT

An Australian ranger took a photo of a ball of lightning. **'Ball lightning'** can be hot enough to boil away water and burn flesh. It can also enter a room. But can it really burn someone to a pile of ash?

NO SMOKE WITHOUT FIRE

Things do not happen without a good reason. That is what science tells us. So why should anyone burn with no flame in sight? In 1980 there were two cases of human **combustion** in cars.

FLORIDA FIRE

Jenna Winchester suddenly **ignited** in her car in Florida. She beat out the flames with her hands as she screamed, 'Get me out of here!' The car crashed into a pole. Jenna **survived** with 20 per cent of her body covered in burns.

Is ball lightning to blame for some human combustion cases?

Agnes Phillips was 82 when she died from burns in a car in New South Wales, Australia. The fire brigade could not see how the fire started or why she had just gone up in flames.

ball lightning   ball of bright light and energy that floats above the ground

MARCH, 1997

A 76-year-old man was found dead in his living room in Ireland. John O'Connor's **charred** remains were in a chair a long way from the fireplace. Only his head, shoulders and feet were not burnt. There was hardly any damage to the room or his chair. The local priest was on the scene and said it looked just as if somebody had poured petrol into John's lap. The chair was full of his ashes.

A PUZZLE

Scientists say humans cannot just ignite. They think a victim's clothes catch fire somehow and become like the wick of a candle. The body then burns slowly till nothing is left.

THE SCENE OF HUMAN COMBUSTION

Most cases happen indoors:

- soot always covers the ceiling and walls, down to a metre above the floor
- objects above this level show signs of heat damage. For example, there may be melted candles or cracked mirrors
- objects below this line show no damage at all.

charred   black and burned
combustion   burning

45

THE WEIRD AND WONDERFUL

WOMEN WITH ENERGY

- Inga Gaiduchenko from Russia is like a human magnet. It is not just metal objects that stick to her. Pens, china, books and all sorts cling to her body.

- Pauline Shaw from Manchester is electric! She often blows fuses just by walking into the room.

Some people's bodies and minds can do weird things. Their wild **talents** cannot be explained. Some children can hear music once and then play it on the piano from memory. Others can multiply huge numbers in their heads faster than a calculator.

HUMAN CAMERA

Ted Serios said he could take a photo with his mind. If he thought hard enough in front of a blank film, his thoughts printed on it. It may have been a big con, but in 1965, many people saw him take a thought photograph.

How do magicians do this trick? >>

illusion   trick that makes it look like magic has happened

FLOATING

Daniel Home had weird skills, too. Or maybe he was just good at tricks. He was a British magician in the 1800s who could stretch his body by 25 centimetres. In 1852, Home showed he could **levitate**. People saw him rise 30 centimetres above the floor. If they held him they were lifted up, too.

For centuries people have tried to rise off the ground by going into a trance. Peter Sugleris says he can do this with great mind power. He was filmed floating half a metre above his kitchen floor in 1986. Such an act has become part of many televison and stage **illusions**.

Do human magnets exist or is it just another trick?

Daniel Home claimed he could levitate himself 30 centimetres off the ground. ❝❝

HUMAN MAGNETS

Some humans seem to **attract** things to their bodies, from needles to frying pans. Objects stick to their bodies and are hard to remove. It is as if they are magnetic. No one can really explain it.

THE 'HUMAN LIGHTNING CONDUCTOR'

Roy Sullivan, from Virginia, USA, was struck by lightning seven times!

- The first hit was in 1942 and the last in 1977.
- His hair was set alight, he lost his big toenail and his eyebrows.
- His arms, legs, chest and stomach were all burned. But he lived!

Lightning can strike the same place – or person – twice! **∨∨**

LIGHTNING MYSTERIES

Many stories tell of people who have a strange effect on electricity. They either seem to make it or **attract** it. Some people even appear to **conduct** lightning.

There are two common beliefs about lightning:
1. It never strikes the same place twice.
2. No human body or brain will **survive** a hit of 100,000 amps.

But these are wrong.

A BOLT FROM THE BLUE

In 1899 a bolt of lightning killed a man in his garden in Italy. Exactly 30 years later, the same man's son was also struck by lightning and killed. But it did not end there. The man's grandson was also struck by lightning in 1949. Not a lucky family.

Troy Trice was wearing his American football gear when he was struck by lightning. He made a full recovery. **❮❮**

BRITAIN'S BIGGEST STRIKE

In 1995, seventeen people sheltered under a tree at a football match. Wham! They were thrown into the air when lightning struck. Some of them had heart attacks, burst eardrums and burns. They all recovered, but ten had strange burn holes on each toe and on the soles of their feet.

WINBURN CHAPEL, MISSISSIPPI

Betty Hudson seems to attract lightning. It struck her head when she was a child, but she got over it. It destroyed her parents' house in 1957. Her home has been struck three times. One bolt of lightning killed her dog and another wrecked her bedroom. Now Betty just keeps her fingers crossed in a storm!

LIGHTNING CAN BE GOOD FOR YOU!

- Samuel Leffers had bad legs and his eye could not close. In 1806 he was struck by lightning. When he woke up, his legs were better and his eye worked. It was a pity that his hearing had gone!
- Lightning also hit Martin Rockwell. He was stunned, but it cured his **asthma**!

conduct   transmit electricity

FEELING BLUE

In 1934 Anna Manaro fell into a deep sleep and her body began to glow bright blue. Her heart beat faster and her blood shone bright blue through her skin. After a few weeks it stopped and to this day no one can explain the mystery.

> Fireflies can glow in the dark. Maybe some people can do the same.

COLOURFUL MYSTERY

There are reports of humans that behave like **glow worms**. For some unknown reason, people can sometimes glow in the dark. They just light up.

A BRIGHT SPARK

In 1995, 10-year-old Liam Lowsley was a mystery at school. Blue sparks flew off his arms and legs if anyone came close to him. A **professor** thought it was **static electricity** in Liam's clothes after the school had been struck by lightning.

REAL SPARKLE

Cha, from Vietnam, began to glow in the dark in 1997. His body was covered in blue-white spots of light at night. His story was in all the newspapers, so he became a real shining star!

> Static electricity can cause sparks to fly.

WEIRD WORDS   **glow worm**   female beetle that glows in the dark
metallic   looking shiny, behaving like metal

THE GREEN CHILDREN OF WOOLPIT

Around AD 1150, two strange children appeared near Woolpit, England. Farmers found a boy and a girl hiding near a pit. The children spoke an unknown language and their clothes were made of a strange material. Stranger still, their skin was green.

The boy soon died, but the girl grew healthy and her skin lost its green glow. She learned English and told how they had come from a land with no sun, where everyone was green.

The story goes on to say that she grew up and married a local man, but her mystery was never **solved**.

THE GREEN CHILDREN OF BANJOS

In 1887, two small children were found alone near a small town in Spain. But the real mystery was that they wore clothes made of a strange **metallic** cloth... and their skin had an odd green tint. No one ever found where they had come from.

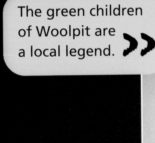

The green children of Woolpit are a local legend. »

professor   expert in a subject who teaches at a university
static electricity   electricity not flowing in a current.

FIND OUT MORE

WEBSITES

GUINNESS WORLD RECORDS

Look under the Human Body section for the most amazing body and mind world records.
guinessworld records.com

BBC SCIENCE

Interactive site with games and quizzes to find out all about your body and mind.
bbc.co.uk/science/ humanbody/

BOOKS

Fortean Times Book of Medical Mayhem,
    Ian Simmons *et al* (John Brown, 1999)
Out There? Mysterious Urban Myths,
    John Townsend (Raintree, 2004)
World of Strange Phenomena Omnibus,
    Charles Berlitz (Warner Books, 1995)

WORLD WIDE WEB

If you want to find out more about **mysteries of body and mind,** you can search the Internet using keywords like these:

- human + magnet
- 'human combustion'
- 'brain waves' + sleep
- 'out of body experience'
- DNA

Make your own keywords by using headings or words from this book.

SEARCH TIPS

There are billions of pages on the Internet so it can be difficult to find exactly what you are looking for. If you just type in 'body' on a search engine like Google, you will get a list of 56 million web pages. These search skills will help you find useful websites more quickly:

- Know exactly what you want to find out about first
- Use two to six keywords in a search, putting the most important words first
- Be precise – only use names of people, places or things
- If you want to find words that go together, put quote marks around them, for example 'extra sensory perception'
- Use the advanced section of your search engine
- Use the + sign to add certain words.

WHERE TO SEARCH

SEARCH ENGINE

looks through the entire web and lists all the sites that match the words in the search box. They can give thousands of links, but the best matches are at the top of the list, on the first page. Try **bbc.co.uk/search**

SEARCH DIRECTORY

A search directory is more like a library of websites that have been sorted by a person instead of a computer. You can search by keyword or subject and browse through the different sites in the same way you would look through books on a library shelf. A good example is **yahooligans.com**

GLOSSARY

acid type of chemical

ancient from a long time ago

antibiotics drugs that fight infection

apparent seeming to be the case

asthma illness that makes breathing difficult

attract pull something towards itself

ball lightning ball of bright light and energy that floats above the ground

bizarre very strange or weird

Buddhist monk man who devotes his life to following the religion of Buddha

cells tiny 'building blocks' that make up all living things

charred black and burnt

coincidence two or more strange things that happen at the same time or together

coma very deep sleep where the brain cannot be woken

combustion burning

conduct transmit electricity

convicted found guilty of a crime

declare announce news in an official way

desire longing or craving for something

DNA code locked in our genes that makes us who we are

Extra Sensory Perception ability to pick up mental signals

evidence information available to help prove if something is true or false

exhausted weak from being very tired and losing all energy

exhibit put something on show

experience event in which someone is personally involved

fatal causing or ending in death

fragile easily broken or damaged

freak show place where people with unusual bodies used to be put on show

gene set of instructions inside every cell

glow worm female beetle that glows in the dark

hormone chemical in the body that makes things happen

hypnosis putting someone into a trance or sleep

ignite catch fire

illusion trick that makes it looks like magic has happened

insomnia inability to sleep

irrational for no clear reason

levitate rise up off the ground and float in the air

magnetic having the power to attract objects

medical science study of diseases, their treatment and the workings of the body

mental to do with the mind

metallic looking shiny, behaving like metal

mind-boggling hard to understand, baffling

miracle something extraordinary or supernatural

mortuary room where dead bodies are kept before they are buried

myth made-up tale, told over the years and handed on

phobia real fear and dread of a particular thing or place

pollen powdery substance from flowers

pope head of the Roman Catholic Church

post mortem examination of a dead body to find the cause of death

pressure force per unit of area

professor expert in a subject who teaches at a university

protein chemical substance in all living cells

psychic showing unusual powers of the mind

puzzle difficult and confusing problem

remain stay the same or be left behind

revive bring back to life

root real reason or cause

scorch burn and brown the surface only

skin graft transplant of skin from another part of the body

solve find the answer

static electricity electricity not flowing in a current

surgery operation in hospital

survive stay alive despite the dangers

survivor someone who lives through a dangerous experience

talent special skill or gift

trance sleep-like state

typical usual example

undertaker person who arranges funerals

unique only one of its kind in the whole world

urgent needing quick action

vital really important

INDEX